Weather

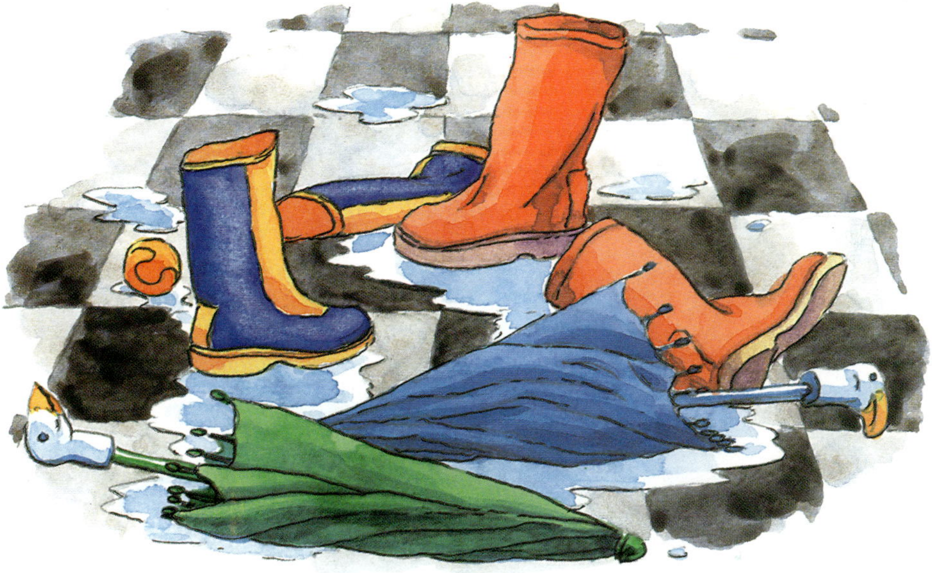

Story by Rod Theodorou
Illustrations by Sue Porter

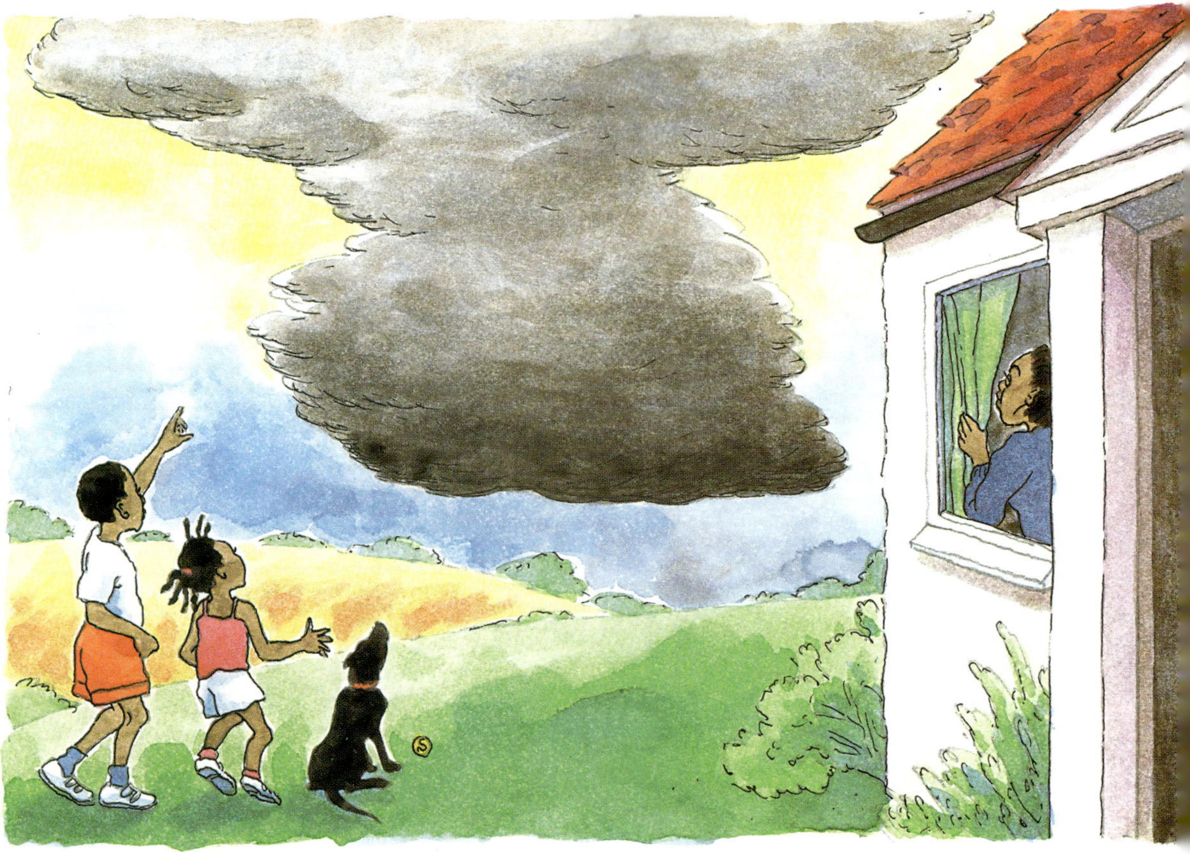

The cloud,

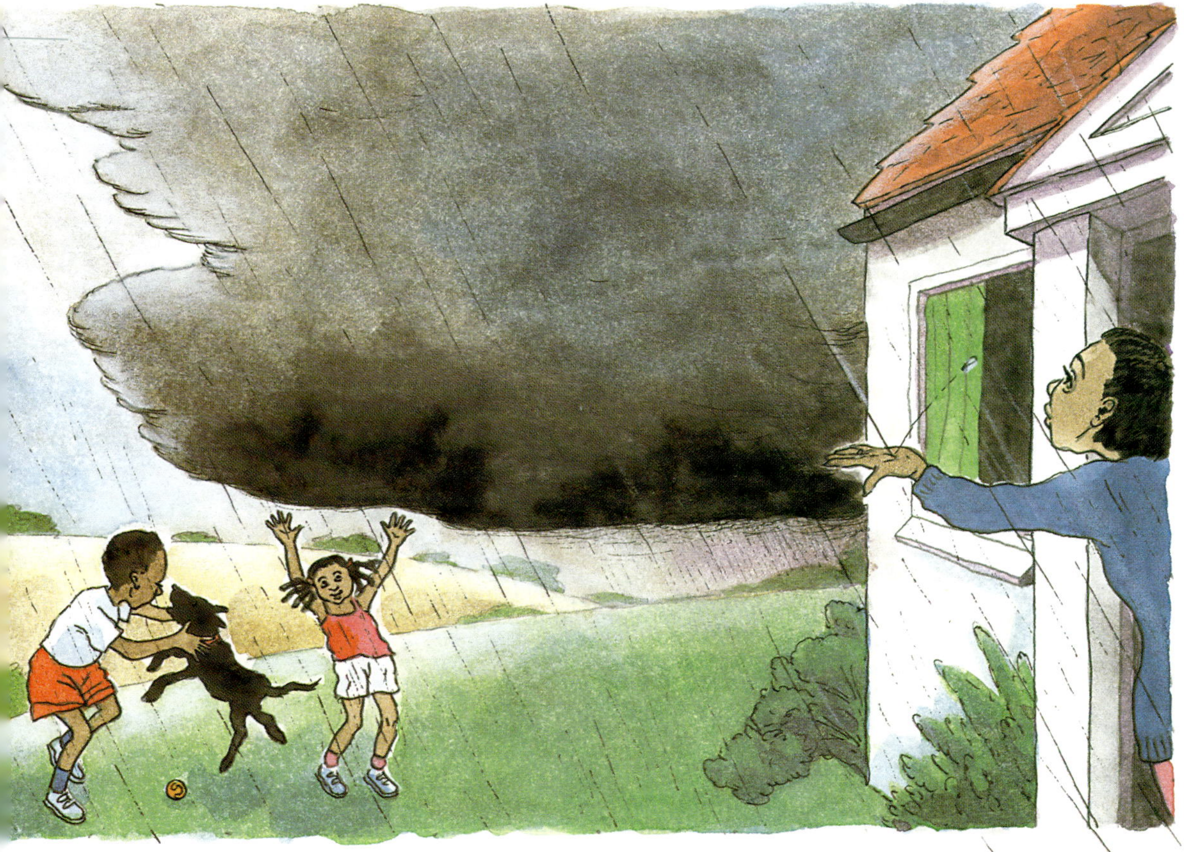

the rain,

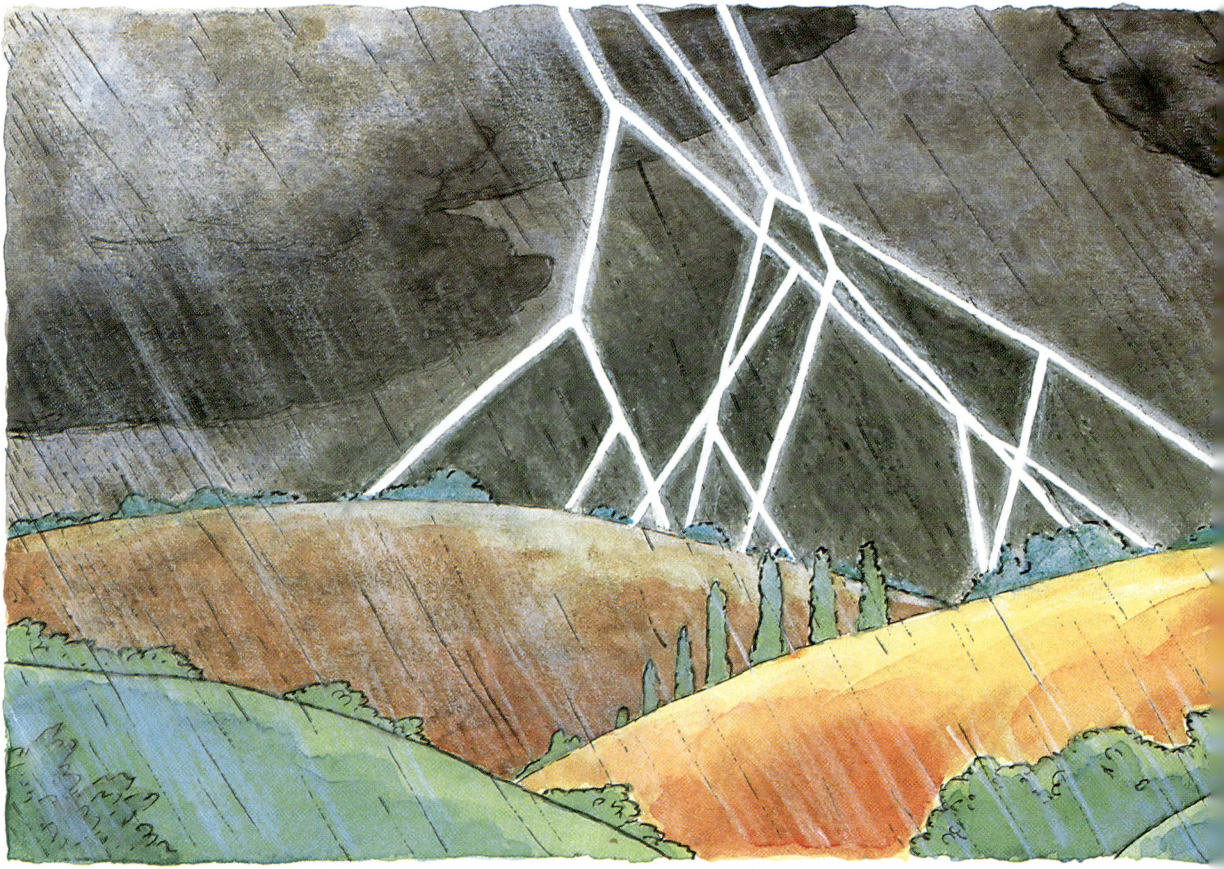

the lightning,

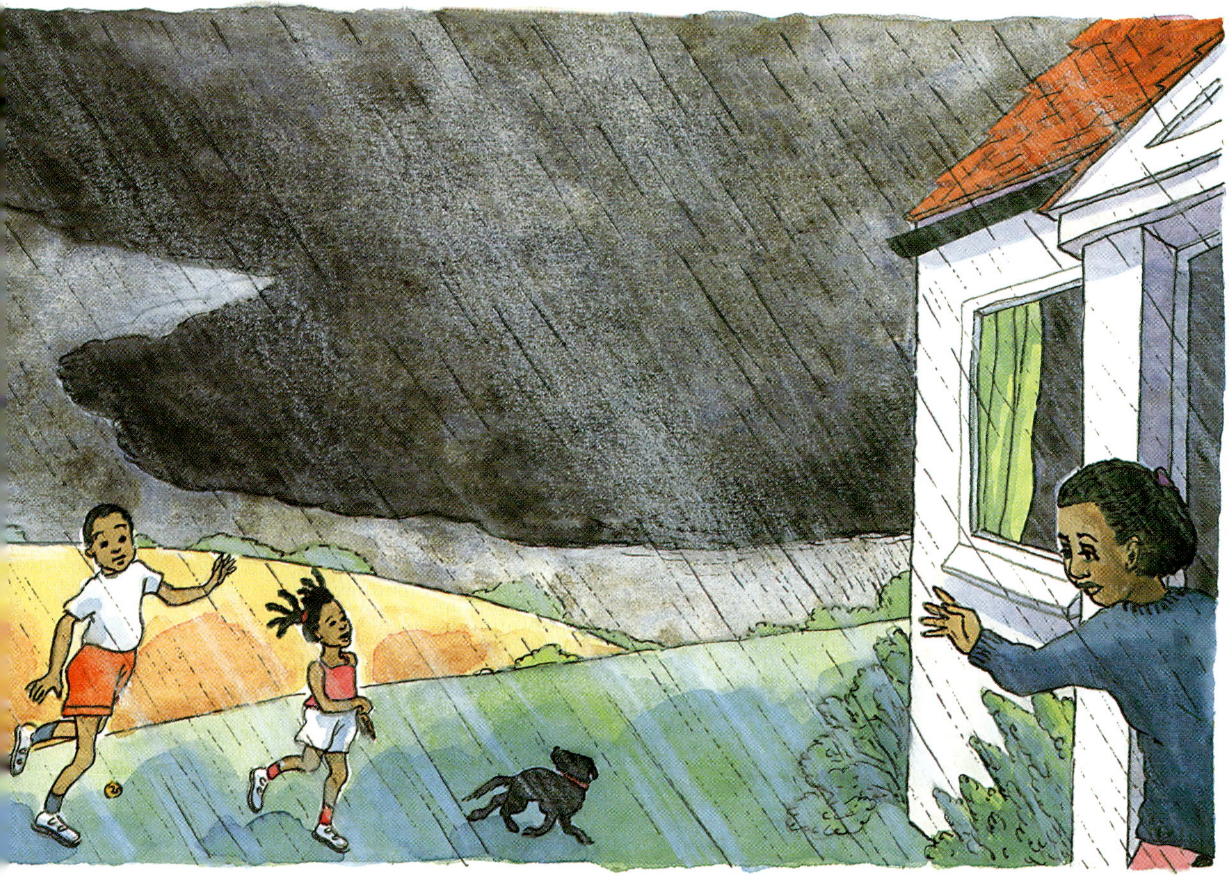

the storm!

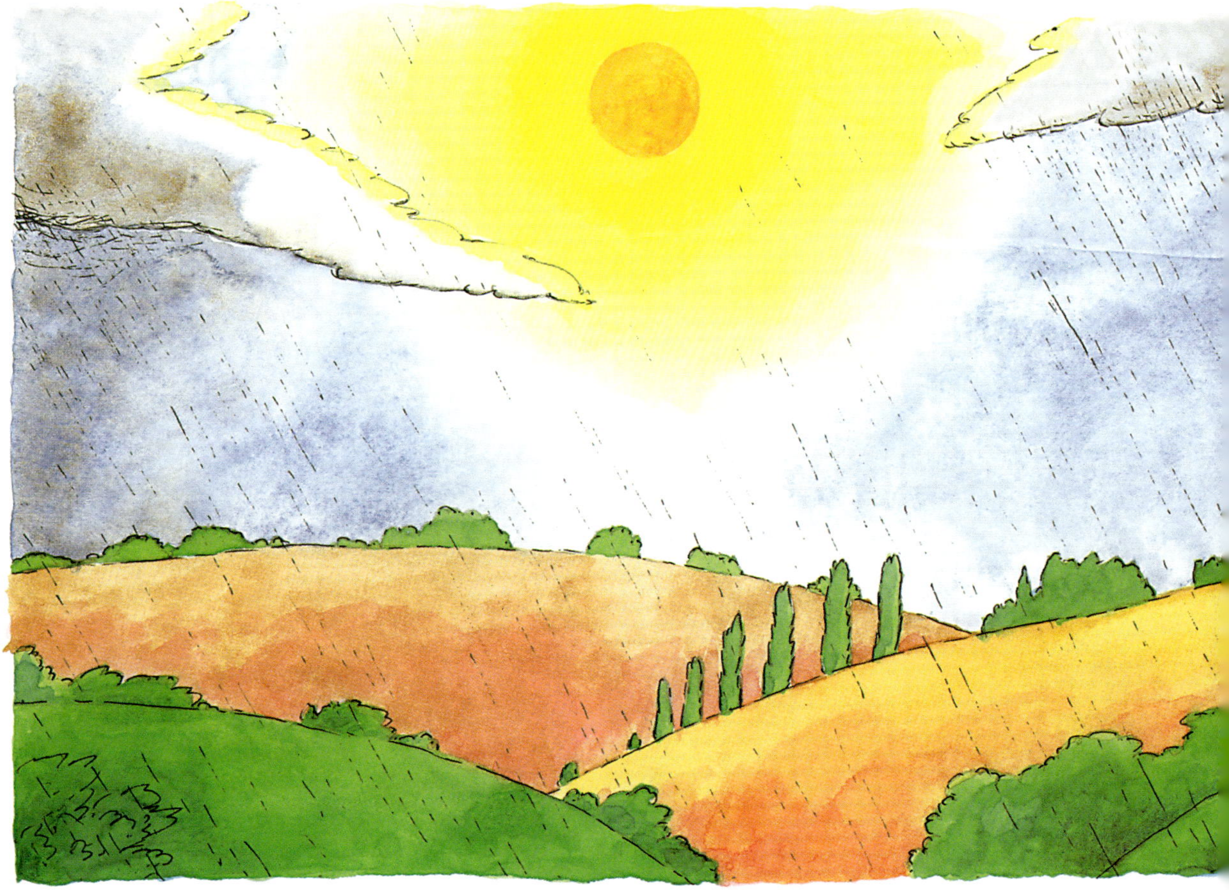

The sun,

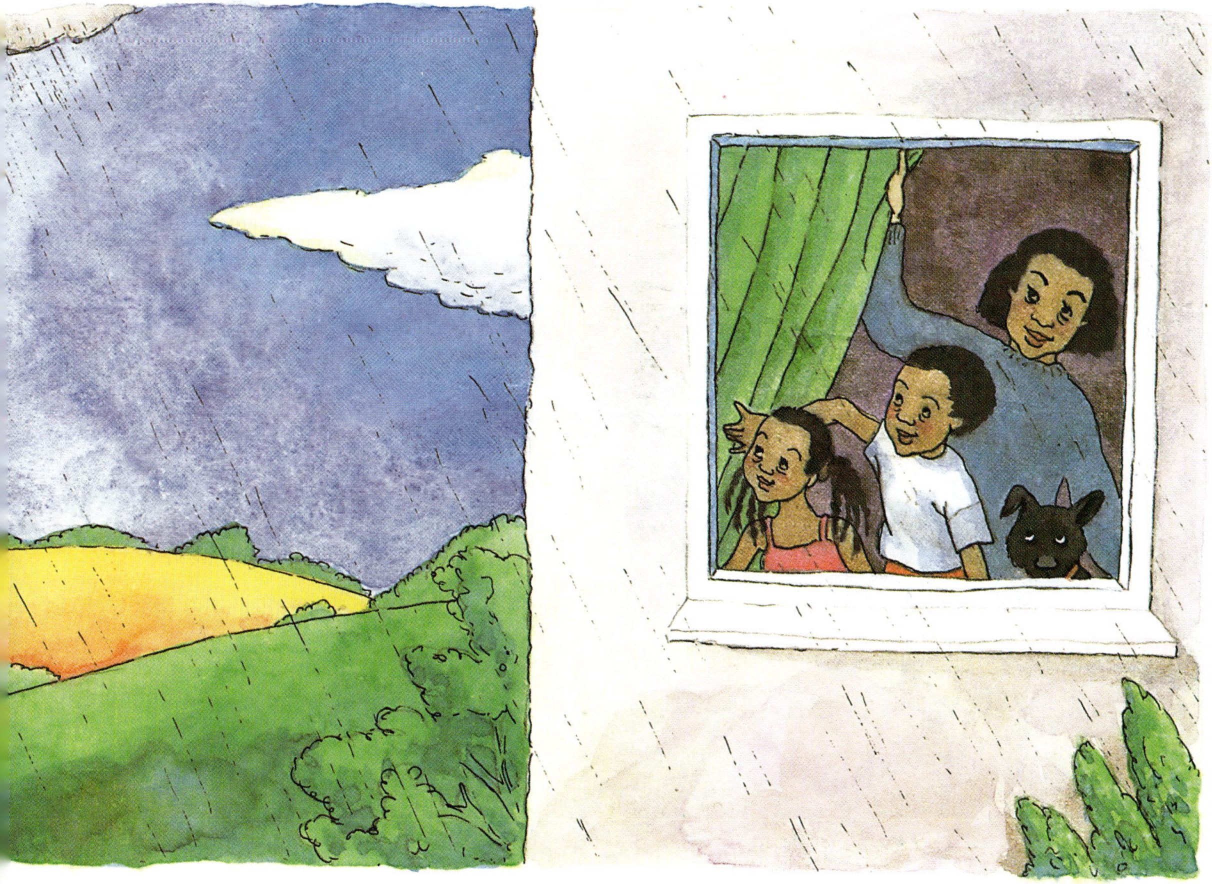

the sky ...

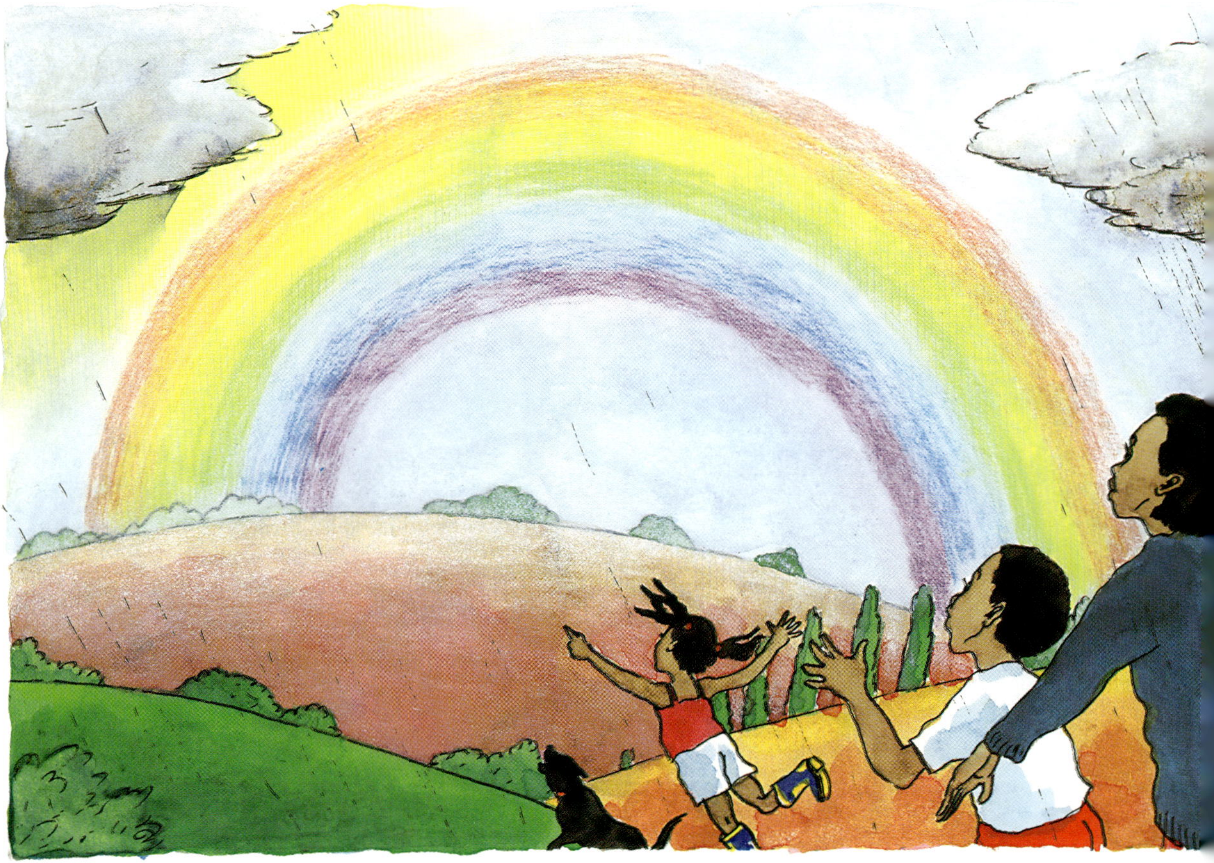

the rainbow!